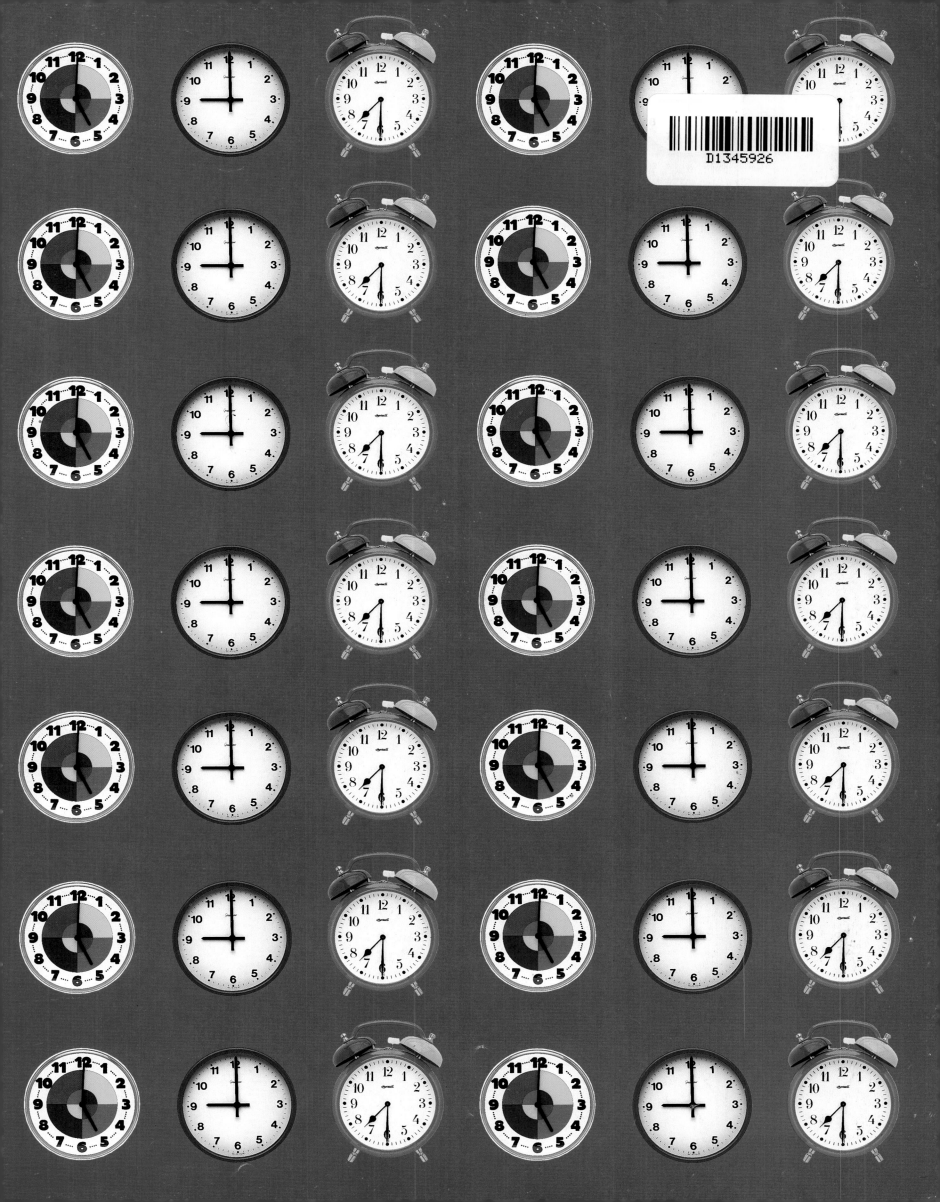

DK First Time Book

Claire Llewellyn

LONDON • NEW YORK • SYDNEY • DELHI

www.dk.com

Editor   Sheila Hanly
Art Editors   Nicki Simmonds, Jane Coney
Senior Art Editor   Rowena Alsey
Production   Marguerite Fenn
Managing Editor   Jane Yorke
Art Director   Roger Priddy

Photography by   Paul Bricknell
Illustrations by   Julie Carpenter

Mathematics consultant   Marie Heinst

First published in Great Britain in 1992
by Dorling Kindersley Limited,
9 Henrietta Street, London, WC2E 8PS
Reprinted 1992, 1993, 1994, 1996, 1997, 1999
Copyright © 1992, 1999 Dorling Kindersley Limited, London

A CIP catalogue record for this book is
available from the British Library

ISBN 0-7513-6307-3

Colour reproduction by Colourscan.
Printed and Bound in TWP SDN. BHD.

Contents

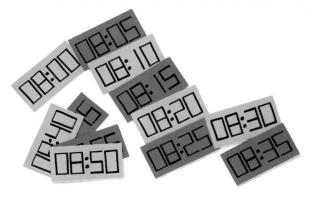

Note to parents and teachers

Time is a difficult concept for children to understand. They cannot see or feel time. The same period seems to pass quickly or slowly, depending on what activity they are engaged in.

A sense of time

Children usually develop a sense of time through becoming familiar with the sequence of events in their daily and weekly routines. They also learn to read clues in their environment that indicate a passage of time, such as seasonal changes in the natural world. By sharing this book and looking at the pages together, you can help your child to develop a sense of time. The wealth of pictures, lively questions, and entertaining puzzles and activities encourage young children to learn through play.

Telling the time

Children want to learn to tell the time. Once mastered, it is a skill that gives them a feeling of competence and independence. However, learning to read a clock is not straightforward. First, children need to have a basic understanding of several mathematical concepts: they must know the number symbols and their sequence; possess an understanding of fractions (eg half past nine) and a sense of equivalency (eg 7:00 is also seven o'clock); and be familiar with the five-times table. The time-telling spreads in this book provide a clear and helpful approach to learning to tell the time. You can help to make the times shown on the pages more meaningful by relating them to your child's own daily routine.

Fun time

Don't expect your child to be able to read the time instantly. The age at which children begin to tell the time with any confidence varies enormously, and they will need lots of practice in order to gain this confidence. Use the fold-out clock to make practising fun. With your help, your child will find this introduction to time-telling an enjoyable learning experience.

Marie Heinst
Mathematics consultant

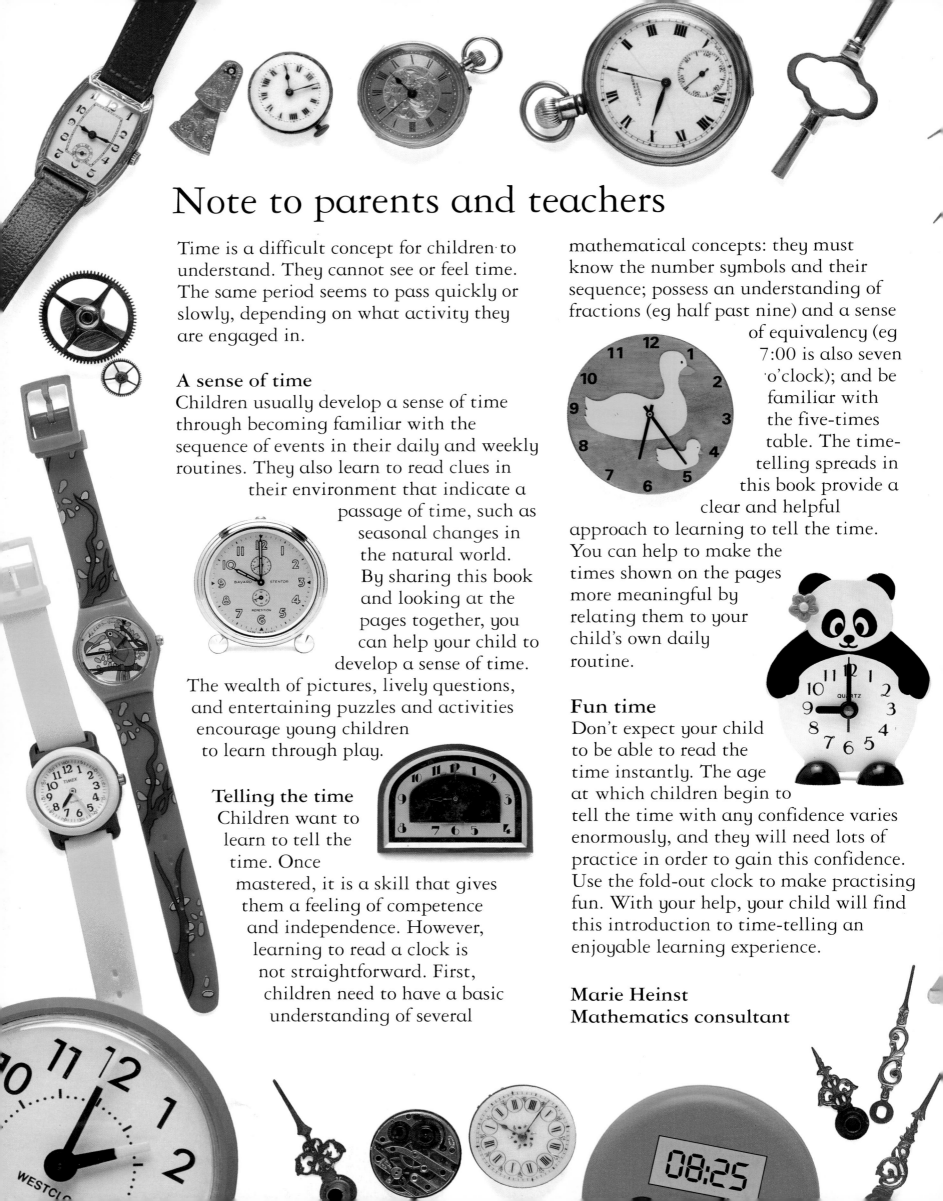

About this book

This book has some special features to help you to learn all about time.

Using your fold-out clock

Inside the back cover of the book, you will find a fold-out clock. You can use it to practise telling the time. It folds out next to any page you are reading.

Your clock has two moveable hands. The short hand is red. It tells you the hours. The long hand is blue. It tells you the minutes. These colours match the hands and numbers of the teaching clocks on the time-telling pages.

Remember, you can practise on your fold-out clock without your book, too.

Spot the clock!

 Look out for this picture on the pages of this book. It tells you when your fold-out clock can help you to solve a puzzle.

Words about time

As you work through the book, you will notice that some words have been highlighted in **heavier print**. These words are explained in **Words about time** on page 32.

Day and night

A new **day** begins each **morning** with the sunrise. We are active during the **daytime** – moving, working, playing, and eating. What do you like to do best during the day?

It begins to get dark each **evening** at sunset. It's difficult to see at **night**, and we need to rest. Almost everyone goes to sleep. Can you think of any people who are awake at night?

Spot the difference

There are many differences between day and night. Look at the two pictures below.

How can you tell which picture shows day and which night?

6

All in a day

Birthdays are the most wonderful days. But they take a whole year to come round and then they seem to be over in a flash! Which is your favourite part of a birthday?

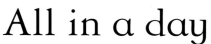

Morning

Is morning the best part, when you get ready for your party?

Afternoon

Do you enjoy the **afternoon** most, when all your friends come to the party?

Evening

Is the evening of your birthday your favourite part? By then, everyone has gone home and you can look back over the whole happy day.

7

Days of the week

Days pass quickly. We join them up to make **weeks**. There are seven days in a week. Do you know their names? This **diary** shows all the special things Rebecca did in one week. What things do you do every week?

Monday

I went on a nature walk during school **today**. Tom and I found some interesting leaves.

Tuesday

We used our leaves from **yesterday** to make a picture. It was a bit messy, but lots of fun.

Wednesday

I always enjoy Wednesdays. It's when I go swimming with my friends.

Thursday

After school I went to cookery club. I made ginger biscuits. Yummy!

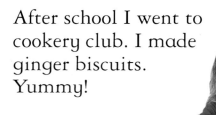

Friday

At band practice today, I kept playing at the wrong time. I'll have to practise for next week.

Saturday

It's the **weekend**. I went shopping with Mum and Dad to buy things for a picnic **tomorrow**.

Sunday

We were out the whole day. It was lovely! Tomorrow is Monday. I wonder if something exciting will happen?

The months of a year

We join about four weeks together to make a **month**. There are 12 months in all. Do you know their names? Not all months are the same length. Some have an extra day or two. There are usually 365 days in a **year**. But every four years there is a **leap year** with an extra day – 29 February.

Number of days in a month			
January	31	July	31
February	28	August	31
March	31	September	30
April	30	October	31
May	31	November	30
June	30	December	31

A calendar month

Have you ever seen a **calendar**? Calendars show all the days of a month on one page. We write on a calendar to remind ourselves of the important things we plan to do in a month. Why not try to make your own calendar?

Making your calendar

1 Gather together the things you will need. Draw lines on the paper, as shown in the picture.

2 Write the name of the month at the top of the paper.

3 Fill in the days of the week. Check how many days there are in your month. Then, fill in the numbers for the days. Remember, months don't always begin on Sunday.

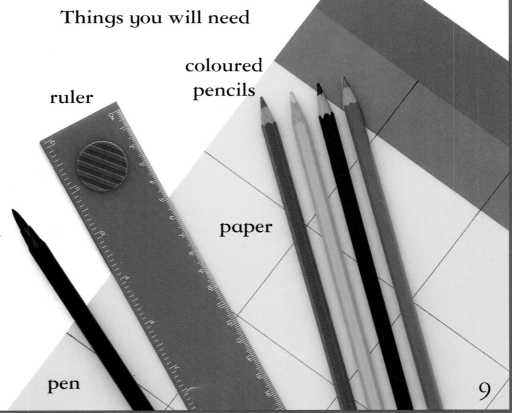

JANUARY						
SUN	MON	TUES	WED	THURS	FRI	SAT
		1	2	3	4	5
6	7	8	9	10	11	12
13	14	15	16	17	18	19
20	21	22	23	24	25	26
27	28	29	30	31		

Things you will need

coloured pencils

ruler

paper

Picture dates

You can mark special **dates** on your calendar by drawing pictures instead of writing.

Birthday   Dentist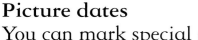

Holiday  A day out

Haircut   Sport

Here are a few picture examples for you to copy. Try to think up some of your own too.

pen

9

The four seasons

Spring, summer, autumn, winter – these are the four seasons that make up our year. Each season brings a number of changes: the weather is different, the daylight is different, the length of each day is different. These changes are very important. All living things notice them, and they begin to change, too.

The changing seasons

- Which is your favourite season?
- What happens to most trees and plants in spring?
- How do animals prepare for winter?
- In which season do most farmers harvest their crops?
- How do you like to keep cool on a hot summer's day?
- Which season comes after winter?

Spring

Spring days are longer and warmer than the cold, dark days of winter. Everything begins to grow. Many animals have babies now.

Summer

In summer, days are long and nights are short. The weather is usually dry and hot. It's the perfect weather for enjoying yourself out-of-doors.

Why do the seasons change?

The top half of the Earth is warm and bright because it's tilted towards the Sun. It's summer here.

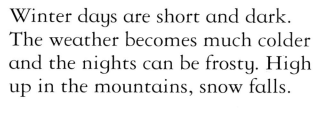

Earth

Sun

The bottom half of the Earth is cold and dark because it's further away from the Sun. It's winter here.

Although we can't feel it, the Earth is always turning. It takes 24 hours to make one full turn. In this picture of the Earth and Sun, one side of the Earth is facing the Sun. It's daytime there. The other side is dark and shaded. It's night-time there.

As it turns, the Earth also circles the Sun. It takes a year to go round the Sun once. In this picture you can see how the Earth is tilted to one side. The top is tilted towards the Sun and it's summer here. As the Earth moves round the Sun, the bottom tilts towards the Sun and the seasons change.

Autumn

Autumn days are shorter and cooler. The leaves on most trees change colour and fall to the ground. Have you ever noticed what the birds do in autumn?

Winter

Winter days are short and dark. The weather becomes much colder and the nights can be frosty. High up in the mountains, snow falls.

Time to grow

All living things grow, and as they grow, they change. Observing these changes in the things around us is one way of noticing that time has passed.

Not everything takes the same amount of time to grow. Some things grow and change very quickly, while others take much longer.

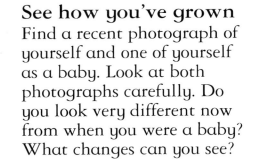

See how you've grown
Find a recent photograph of yourself and one of yourself as a baby. Look at both photographs carefully. Do you look very different now from when you were a baby? What changes can you see?

Days to grow

mung beans

after one day

after six days

You shouldn't eat bean sprouts that have grown as big as these.

Try this experiment to see how quickly mung beans grow. Soak a handful of mung beans overnight in a jar of water. Drain them well and leave the jar in a warm place.

Rinse the beans daily with clean water. After two days they should start to sprout. In six days, the bean sprouts will have grown roots and leaves.

Weeks to grow

Ducklings grow at a slower pace than beans. The tiny one-day-old duckling is covered in fluffy down. After two weeks its feathers start to grow. At eight weeks, the duck is fully grown.

one day old

two weeks old

eight weeks old

Years to grow

People grow so slowly that we usually measure their growth in years, not in weeks or days. A year is a long time. It's the amount of time between one birthday and the next. Look at these pictures of a woman at different ages throughout her life.

- How has this woman changed over the years?
- What other living things take years to grow?
- How old are you?
- How many years do you think it will take for you to become a grown-up?

1 year old   4 years old   14 years old   27 years old   58 years old

Birthday puzzle

Each candle on a birthday cake stands for one year of someone's life. Count the candles on these birthday cakes.

Try to work out how old the children are. Can you put them in order of their ages? How old will you be on your next birthday?

Rebecca   Billy   Tom   Jane

- Who is the oldest child in these pictures?
- Who is the youngest child?
- Is Tom or Billy older than Rebecca?

- Can you work out how old Tom will be on his next birthday?
- Is Billy older or younger than you?

13

A world of clocks

We use **clocks** and **watches** to tell the time. Once you begin to notice them, you will spot clocks everywhere. Can you imagine what it would be like if we had no clocks to help us keep track of time? All the clocks on these pages have special jobs. Can you think of other useful clocks?

Airport clock
If you don't check the time on the airport clock, you might miss your plane.

Nurse's watch
Nurses wear these watches pinned to their uniforms. Why do you think the face hangs upside down?

Video clock
Why do we need a clock on a video recorder?

Digital clock
What do you think makes this digital clock work?

Picture clock
Brightly coloured clocks are made specially for younger children.

Wind-up clock
You can see the insides of this carriage clock. It has a glass door at the back, so you can watch the moving parts. It also has a special key to wind it up to make it go.

Digital watch
Can you see what makes this digital watch work?

Oven clock
The clock on an oven has a buzzer that helps us to remember to take food out of the oven before it burns!

14

Station clock
A clock at a railway station tells people when to catch their trains.

Cuckoo clock
Every hour a bird pops out of a door at the top of this clock and says "cuckoo".

Floral clock
This clock's numbers are made of plants! Where might you see a clock like this?

Alarm clock
How does an alarm clock help to wake you in the morning?

Clocks on buildings
There are beautiful and interesting old clocks on different buildings all over the world. Is there a special clock on a building in the town where you live? What types of building often have clocks on them?

Modern clock
It's difficult to tell the time on this clock. It doesn't have any numbers!

Grandfather clock
This grandfather clock is very tall. It makes a loud "tick-tock" noise. Do you know what sort of noise it makes every hour?

Child's watch
The numbers are easy to read on this watch. It helps you to learn to tell the time.

On the hour

Most clocks have two hands to tell you the time. The two hands move slowly round the **clockface**. The **short hand** tells you the **hour**. It takes 12 hours for the short hand to go all the way round the clockface. The **long hand** tells you the **minutes**. It takes one hour to move round the clockface.

eleven o'clock

twelve o'clock

one o'clock

two o'clock

When the long hand is pointing straight up at the 12, it tells you that it's something **o'clock**.

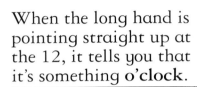

The short hand is pointing to the 8.

Together, the hands tell you that the time is eight o'clock.

ten o'clock

three o'clock

nine o'clock

four o'clock

The hands on a clock always move in the same direction – we call it **clockwise**.

eight o'clock

seven o'clock

six o'clock

five o'clock

These clocks show every hour of the day.
• Can you tell the different times?

• What were you doing at these times today?
• Which is your favourite hour of the day?

Digital time

A **digital clock** doesn't have a face and it doesn't have any hands. It uses numbers to tell us the time.

The number before the dots tells you which hour it is, just like the short hand on an ordinary clock. The number after the dots tells you the minutes. It's like the long hand on an ordinary clock.

- Are there any digital clocks in your house?
- Where else can you find digital clocks?

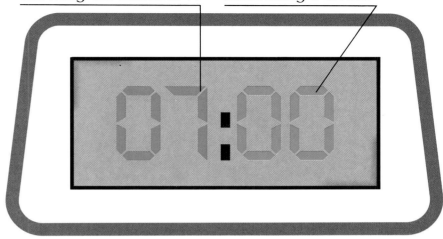

This number tells you which hour it is. It's showing the number 7.

This number tells you the minutes. It's showing 00, which means it's something o'clock.

Together, the numbers tell you that the time is seven o'clock.

Matching time

- What times do all these clocks and watches show?
- Can you find the clocks that show the same time?
- Try to move the hands of your fold-out clock to match all the times shown on this page.

17

Halves and quarters

Have you ever heard people say, "It's half past six," or "It's a quarter to three"? Do you know what they mean? It's the long hand on a clock that tells us about the halves and quarters. It takes one hour for the long hand to go all the way round the clockface.

to • past

Past and to

When the long hand moves between the 12 and the 6, we say the time is past the hour. When the long hand moves between the 6 and the 12, we say the time is to the hour.

Quarter past

When the long hand is on the 3, it's gone a quarter of the way round the clockface. We say it's a **quarter past**. The short hand is just past the 8, so the time is a quarter past eight.

Half past

When the long hand is on the 6, it has gone halfway round the clockface. We say it's **half past**. The short hand is halfway between the 8 and 9, so the time is half past eight.

Quarter to

When the long hand is on the 9, it has gone three quarters of the way round the clockface. It has one more quarter to go. We say it's a **quarter to**. What time does this clock show?

Tell the time

Practise telling the time on these clocks and watches.

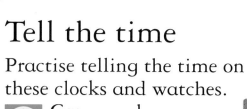 Can you show these times on your fold-out clock?

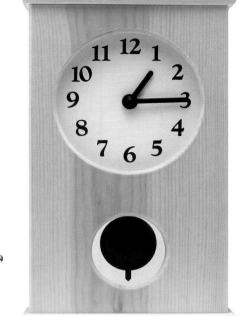

Start to finish

Half an hour and a quarter of an hour are useful terms when we talk about time. Look at the clocks and work out how long Anna takes to make her mask.

start

finish

1 First, Anna traces the shape of the mask and cuts it out. How long does she take?

start

finish

2 Next, Anna draws patterns on the mask. How much time has passed since Anna started making her mask?

start

finish

3 Last of all, Anna sticks everything together. Her mask is finished. How long, in total, has it taken Anna to make her mask?

19

Minutes and seconds

An hour is a long time. A **minute** is much shorter. There are 60 minutes in an hour. The minutes are marked round the edge of the clockface.

There are five minutes between each number on a clockface. The clocks below show the minute hand travelling through one hour in five-minute steps.

five to three

two o'clock

five past two

ten past two

ten to three

The long hand is on the 11. It has gone round 55 minutes. There are five minutes of the hour to go.

There are 5 minutes between each number on a clockface.

The short hand is nearly on the 9.

Together, the two hands tell you that the time is five minutes to nine o'clock or, as we usually say, five to nine.

quarter to three

quarter past two

twenty past two

twenty to three

twenty-five to three

half past two

twenty-five past two

• What happens to the short hand as the long hand moves round the clockface?

• Try counting to 60 in fives – it's easy once you know how!

20

Seconds

Seconds are very short. There are 60 of them in one minute. You can't do much in a second – just sneeze, perhaps, or clap your hands. Some clocks and watches count out the seconds with an extra hand that moves very quickly round the clockface. Do you have any clocks with second hands in your home?

- Why do we need seconds?
- When do we use seconds to measure time?

second hand

Just a second
See if you can beat a drum or clap your hands 10 times in 10 seconds. Check on a clock with a second hand. Were you too fast, too slow, or just right?

Find the pairs

For each of the times written below, there is a matching time on a clock or watch.

When you find a pair, cover the two boxes with coins or small pieces of paper.

(clock image)	**Twenty past one**	*(bear cloud clock image)*	**Ten to eleven**	*(watch image)*
Twenty-five to ten	*(clock image)*	**Five to four**	*(Lorus clock image)*	**Twenty to three**
(watch image)	**Ten past nine**	*(alarm clock image)*	**Five past seven**	*(clock image)*
Twenty-five past three	*(Lorus alarm clock image)*	**Twenty to eight**	*(duck clock image)*	**Ten to six**

Digital clocks

Digital clocks use numbers to tell the time. The numbers before the dots tell you the hour. They go from 1 to 12.

The numbers after the dots tell you the minutes. These go from 1 to 60. Can you think why?

Halves and quarters

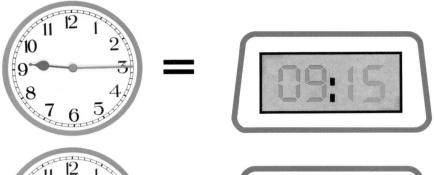

Quarter past
It's a quarter past nine. On the ordinary clock, the long hand has gone round 15 minutes. The digital clock shows 09:15. But we don't say fifteen past nine. What do we usually say?

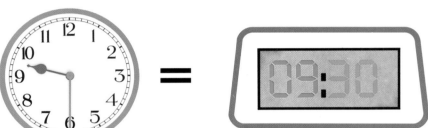

Half past
It's half past nine. On the ordinary clock, the long hand has gone round 30 minutes. The digital clock shows 09:30. How do we usually say this time?

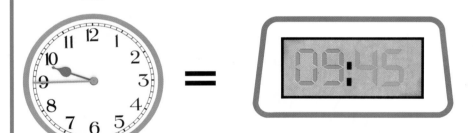

Quarter to
It's a quarter to ten. On the ordinary clock, the long hand has gone round 45 minutes. The digital clock shows 09:45. How do we usually say this time?

Sixty minutes

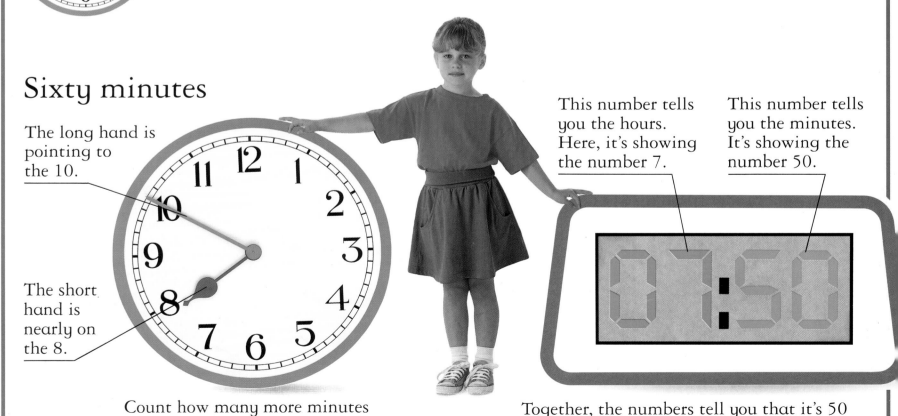

The long hand is pointing to the 10.

The short hand is nearly on the 8.

Count how many more minutes the long hand has to travel before it gets back to the 12.

This number tells you the hours. Here, it's showing the number 7.

This number tells you the minutes. It's showing the number 50.

Together, the numbers tell you that it's 50 minutes past 7, or 7:50. But we can also say it's ten to eight. Can you work out why?

Tell the digital time

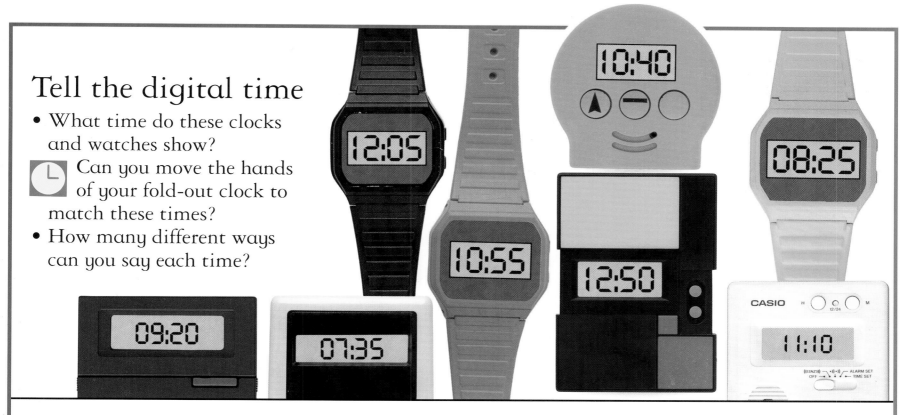

- What time do these clocks and watches show?
- Can you move the hands of your fold-out clock to match these times?
- How many different ways can you say each time?

Clock cards

Here is a fun game to practise telling the time on a digital clock. You can make this game quite easily, or ask a friend to help.

The game can be played by two or four players. It will help you and your friends to practise counting up in fives.

Making your cards

1 On a piece of stiff card, draw 24 rectangles about 14cm wide and 7cm deep. Cut along the lines. Take care when using sharp scissors.

How to play

- Deal out all the cards, so that each player has the same number.
- The first player puts any card face up on the table. The next player tries to lay a card alongside, with a time five minutes earlier or later than the card before.
- Players who can't find a card with the right time on it, miss their turn.
- The winner is the first player with no cards left.

2 Write a digital time on each card. Start at any time, but make sure that each card shows a time five minutes after the card before.

Lay the cards down like this. You can build on either side of the starting card.

The 24-hour clock

Although there are 24 hours in a day, traditional clocks are numbered 1 to 12. In one day, the short hand travels round the clockface twice.

Some digital clocks are different. They number the hours 1 to 24. This way of telling the time is called the 24-hour clock.

The time is eight o'clock. But is it eight o'clock in the morning or in the evening? An ordinary clock doesn't say. But this special clock also shows the hours up to 24.

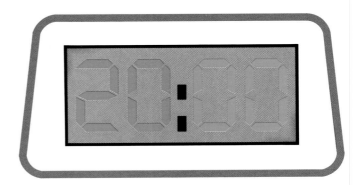

The time is eight o'clock. A digital clock is quite clear – it is eight o'clock in the evening.

Time line

On a 24-hour clock, you start counting the hours from **midnight**. Up until **midday**, the hours are numbered 1 to 12. After midday they are numbered 13 to 24.

midnight   midday   midnight

a.m.   p.m.

24:00 01:00 02:00 03:00 04:00 05:00 06:00 07:00 08:00 09:00 10:00 11:00 12:00 13:00 14:00 15:00 16:00 17:00 18:00 19:00 20:00 21:00 22:00 23:00 24:00

Morning or afternoon?
You don't have to use the 24-hour clock to show whether a time is in the morning or the afternoon. You can use letters instead. We use **a.m.** to show that it's before midday, and **p.m.** to show that it's after midday.

After midday

The 24-hour clock may number the hours 1 to 24, but we don't say half past thirteen. We say half past one instead. All of these clocks and watches show times after 12 o'clock, midday.
• Can you read these times and show them on your fold-out clock?

24

Time around the world

The Earth is always turning. So, as the day begins and the Sun rises on one side of the world, the same day ends and the Sun sets on the opposite side of the world. Isn't it amazing to think that when you're eating breakfast, it's still night in America and most children there are asleep?

Time zones

Because of these big differences in time, the world has been divided up into 24 different time zones, one for each hour of the clock. Can you count the zones on this map?

Flying across time zones

Planes can take off in one time zone and land in a different one. Passengers have to change their watches to the new time.

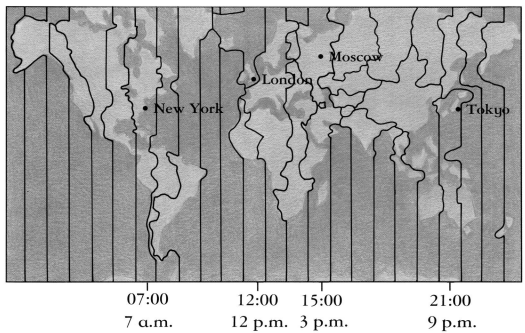

| 07:00 | 12:00 | 15:00 | 21:00 |
| 7 a.m. | 12 p.m. | 3 p.m. | 9 p.m. |

A single moment

Many children live a similar life to yours all over the world. But at exactly the same moment, they may be doing very different things. What would you be doing at the same times as these children from different places in the world?

7 a.m.
07:00

New York, USA
In New York it's seven o'clock in the morning. Bobby is getting dressed. He's got a busy day ahead of him.

London, Great Britain
In London it's midday. Rebecca is hungry. What's in her packed lunch today?

12 p.m.
12:00

3 p.m.
15:00

Moscow, Russia
In Moscow it's three o'clock in the afternoon. Mikhail is drawing a picture.

9 p.m.
21:00

Tokyo, Japan
In Tokyo it's nine o'clock at night. Yoshimi is fast asleep.

25

Fast and slow

Sometimes, we use clocks to measure the time we take to do things – in a race or a game, perhaps. But you don't always have to use a clock.

There are other ways you can time yourself – with a sand-timer, for example. Why not make one and try timing things for yourself?

The smaller the hole in your cone, the slower the sand will run through.

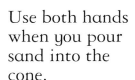

Use both hands when you pour sand into the cone.

Make a sand-timer

1 Draw a rectangle, about 38cm by 18cm, on a piece of card. Cut it out. You should take extra care when using sharp scissors.

2 Roll the card into a cone, leaving a very small hole at the bottom. Stick the cone in place with sticky tape.

3 Put the cone in a large jar. Now, pour some dry sand into the cone. Always use exactly the same amount of sand to time yourself.

Time without numbers

You can use your sand-timer to see how quickly or slowly you do certain things. Count how many times you can write your name, or hop on one foot, before all the sand runs through the timer. Race against a friend or try to beat the timer.

Balancing trick

Try balancing a ball on the soles of your feet. Can you keep it balanced for as long as it takes for the sand to run through the timer?

Speedy skipping

How many times can you skip before the sand runs out? Try to guess before you race the timer. Were you close?

Sweet race

Try picking up sweets from a bowl by sucking through a straw. How many sweets can you drop onto a plate before all the sand runs through?

Counting in seconds

Have you ever seen **timers** like these? Most of them use seconds, minutes, and hours to measure time.

Cooking timer
You can set this timer so that a bell rings when your food is cooked.

Egg timer
When is this timer especially useful?

Stopwatch
Press the button on a stopwatch at the start of a race and again at the end to find out the winner's time.

In a split-second
Stopwatches and digital watches are good for timing races. They count up the time in seconds. Have you ever seen a timer for races on television? Sometimes there is less than one second between two competitors at the finish!

Digital stopwatch
Digital watches have a special timing button. Press it, and the watch begins to count in seconds.

Ready, steady, go!

Why not use a stopwatch to time a race between you and your friends? Don't just run – try hopping, skipping, and jumping. Running may give the quickest time, but what gives the slowest? Try the races again to see if you can do them more quickly.

Back-to-front
Try walking backwards. Is this faster or slower than hopping?

Hop-a-long
Have a hopping race. First, try your right leg, then, your left. Is there a difference in the times?

On three legs
You may need to practise for a three-legged race! See if you can beat your own best time each time you race.

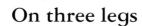

27

Past times

People have measured the passage of time for thousands of years. They first used the movements of the Sun to keep track of time. Have you ever noticed how a shadow from a tree moves during the day? You can tell the position of the Sun in the sky by looking at the length of a shadow.

Be a shadow stick
On a sunny day, mark a spot on the ground and stand on it once every hour. Ask a friend to draw round your shadow each time. What do you notice about the shadow?

Sunshine and shadow

After a time, people used shadows to make a more accurate kind of clock: the sundial. Sundials are found out-of-doors. They are usually placed on the walls of buildings that face the sun, or in the middle of a garden, away from shady trees.

Have you ever seen a sundial?

- When can't you use a sundial to tell the time?

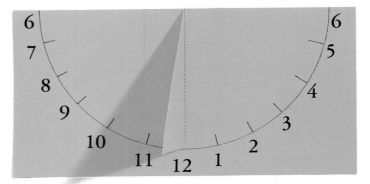

How sundials work
There is a pointer fixed in the middle of a sundial. When the sun shines, the pointer casts a shadow onto the base of the sundial. The markings on the base show us what hour it is.

Wax and water

People thought of other ways of marking the passage of time. They saw that burning candles of the same size took the same amount of time to melt away. They also realized that water would drip from one container into another at a steady rate. Candle and water clocks both work quite well as markers of time, but can you think of any problems you might have with them?

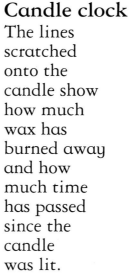

Candle clock
The lines scratched onto the candle show how much wax has burned away and how much time has passed since the candle was lit.

Water clock
The water drips through a small hole, from one container into another. The passing hours are shown by the rising water levels in the container below.

Early clocks and watches

Mechanical clocks were first made about 700 years ago. But only when the pendulum was invented 300 years later, did clocks begin to keep good time. People wanted to be able to tell the time accurately wherever they went. **Watches** became popular, carried in a pocket or as pieces of jewellery. Today, our lives seem to be ruled by time!

Mechanical clock

The clock's tightly coiled springs turn the cogs as they unwind. The cogs make the hands move round the clockface.

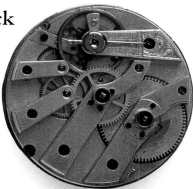

Pocket watch

Pocket watches were used until quite recently. People carry them in their pockets, attached to a chain to keep them safe.

Pendulum clock

A pendulum takes exactly the same amount of time to swing back and forth. Its regular motion moves the clock's hands round accurately.

Wristwatch

People now wear watches on straps so that they can carry and see them easily.

Missing numbers

Today, clocks and watches are made in all kinds of shapes and designs. Some clockfaces don't even have numbers on them!

- Can you tell the time on these modern clocks and watches?

  Move the hands of your fold-out clock to the same times as these clocks and watches to check if you were right.

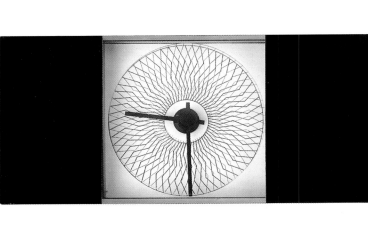

29

Playtime

On these pages there are some fun puzzles for you to solve. You can practise all you've learnt about telling the time.

Follow the lines

- What time does Bobby wake up in the morning?
- When does Joanne leave for school?
- What time is Mark's favourite television programme?
- When does Anna eat her lunch?

Joanne   Bobby   Anna   Mark

How many ways to say. . .?

How many different ways can you say the times shown on these clocks and watches?

Fold-out fun

Try to answer these questions, using your fold-out clock to show the different times.

- What time do you usually wake up in the morning?
- What time does school start?
- What time is break-time?
- What time does school end?
- What time do you usually eat dinner?
- What's the earliest time you've ever been awake?

Roman numerals

Some clocks have numbers that you might not recognize. They are called **Roman numerals**. Have you ever seen a clock or watch with numbers like these on its face? You can use the table below to help you tell the time on these clocks.

I	II	III	*IIII	V	VI
1	2	3	4	5	6
VII	VIII	IX	X	XI	XII
7	8	9	10	11	12

* See note on page 32.

Mix and match

Each of the times shown below has a pair.
How many can you match up?

When you find a pair, cover the two boxes
with coins or small pieces of paper.

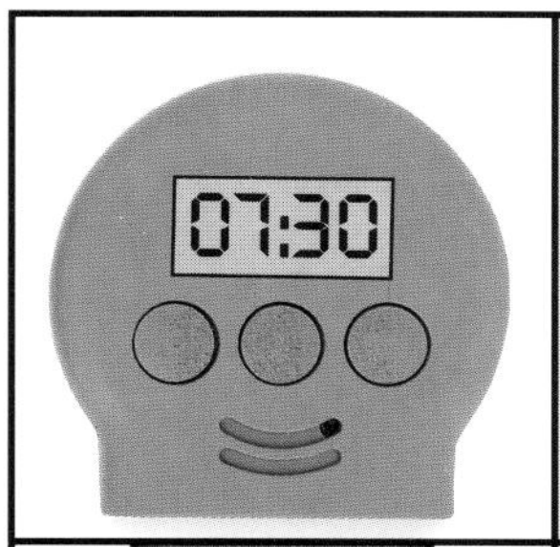 07:30	five to one		 08:25		ten to twelve
 10:50		 11:10		 09:12	
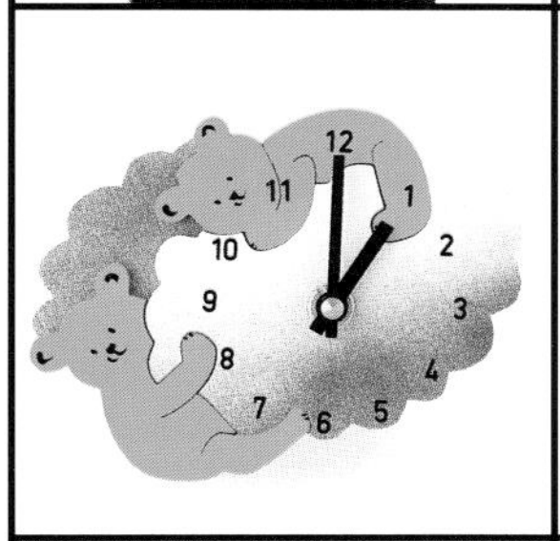		quarter to five			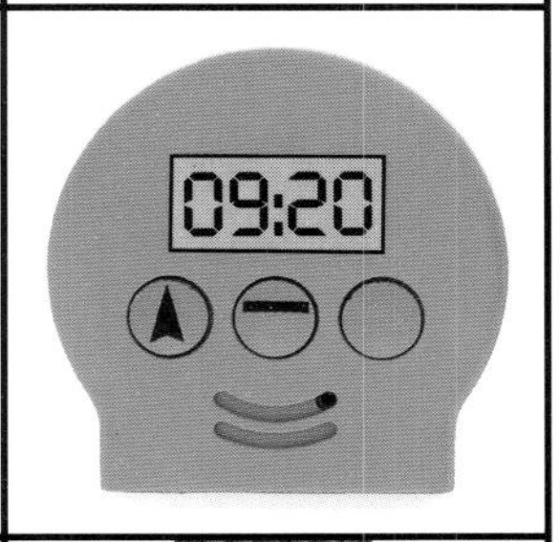 09:20
five past twelve	 08:35			ten to six	
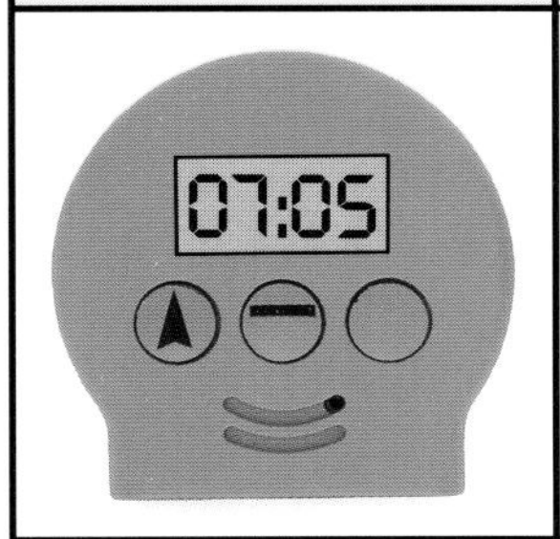 07:05	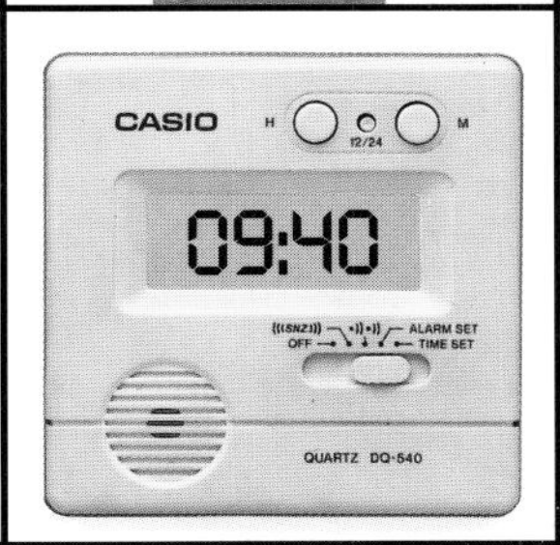 09:40	 11:50	ten past three		 12:05
	twenty-five to six	 10:45		one o'clock	
 17:20		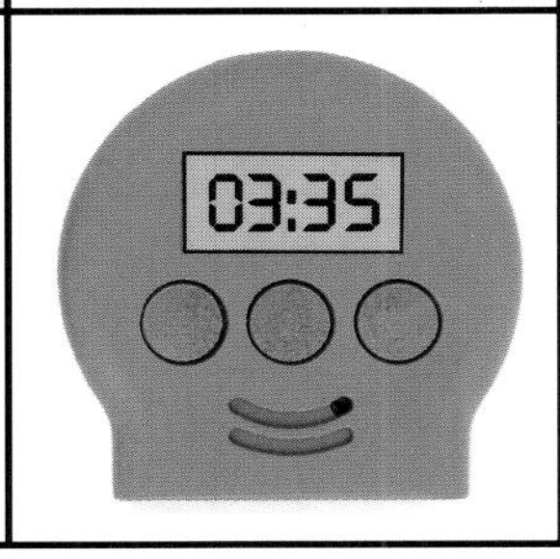 03:35		 05:50	twenty-five past six

Words about time

a.m. These letters stand for the Latin word, *antemeridian*, meaning before midday. (page 24)

afternoon The part of the day between midday and sunset is called afternoon. (page 7)

calendar A calendar shows all the days of the month on one page. You can write down the things you plan to do on certain dates. (page 9)

clock Clocks have hands that move round at a regular pace, to help us keep track of time. (page 14)

clockface The part of a clock where you find the numbers and hands is called the clockface. (page 16)

clockwise The hands of a clock always move in the same direction, following the numbers from 1 to 12. This is called a clockwise direction. (page 16)

date A date is the day, month, and year when something happens. (page 9)

day There are 24 hours in a day. There are 365 days in a year. (page 6)

daytime From sunrise to sunset is daytime. It is light and you can see the sun. (page 6)

diary A diary shows all the days of a year. It has space for you to write down the things you plan to do each day. (page 8)

digital clock Digital clocks and watches show the time with numbers instead of hands. (page 17)

evening The evening is the part of the day when the sun goes down and it gets darker, but it is not yet night. (page 6)

half past Half an hour is 30 minutes. So, half past the hour is 30 minutes after the hour. (page 18)

hour There are 60 minutes in an hour and 24 hours in a day. (page 16)

leap year Every fourth year is called a leap year because an extra day is added. There are 366 days in a leap year. (page 9)

long hand The long hand on a clockface is the minute hand. (page 16)

midday Twelve o'clock in the middle of the day is called midday. (page 24)

midnight Twelve o'clock in the middle of the night is called midnight. (page 24)

minute There are 60 seconds in a minute. There are 60 minutes in an hour. (page 20)

month There are about four weeks in a month. There are 12 months in a year: January, February, March, April, May, June, July, August, September, October, November, and December. (page 9)

morning The part of the day between sunrise and midday is called morning. (page 6)

night From sunset to sunrise is night. It is dark and you can see the moon and stars. (page 6)

p.m. These letters stand for the Latin word, *postmeridian*, meaning after midday. (page 24)

quarter past Quarter of an hour is 15 minutes. So, quarter past the hour is 15 minutes after the hour. (page 18)

quarter to Quarter of an hour is 15 minutes. So quarter to the hour is 15 minutes before the hour is over. (page 18)

Roman numerals Roman numerals are a set of numbers that were used a long time ago by the ancient Romans. We still use these numbers today. You may have seen them on clocks or watches. Roman numerals usually show 4 as IV, but on a clock, 4 is shown as IIII. (page 30)

second There are 60 seconds in a minute. A part of a second is called a split-second. (page 21)

short hand The short hand on a clockface is the hour hand. (page 16)

timer Although a timer looks like a clock, it doesn't tell us the time of day. Instead, it counts in minutes and seconds so that we can measure how long something takes. (page 27)

today Today is the present day – the day it is now. (page 8)

tomorrow Tomorrow is the day after today. It is in the future. (page 8)

watch A watch is a small clock that you can wear on your wrist. (page 14)

week There are seven days in a week: Sunday, Monday, Tuesday, Wednesday, Thursday, Friday, and Saturday. (page 8)

weekend Together, Saturday and Sunday are called the weekend. (page 8)

year There are 12 months in a year. (page 9)

yesterday Yesterday is the day before today. It is in the past. (page 8)

Acknowledgements

Dorling Kindersley would like to thank the following for their help in producing this book:
Steve Shott; Dave King; Mark Richards; Steve Gorton;
Siobhan Power; Anita Ruddell; Neil Morris for writing the
initial synopsis; Snow and Rock for the use of ski equipment and
clothing; Trevor Smith's Animal World; Neil Blaxill for the use
of antique clocks and watches; HS Walsh and Sons Ltd for
the use of clock parts.

**Dorling Kindersley would also like to give special thanks
to the following for appearing in this book:**
Joanne Bacchus; Amy Bradsell; Hannah Capleton; Bobby
Cooper; Benjamin Cowler; Billy Dunne; Sophie Gamba; Daniel
Gregory; Rebecca Kern; William Lindsay; Catherine McAulay;
Mark Natthan; Tebedge Ricketts; Cole Salewicz; Steve Shott;
Beryl Simmonds; Dawn Sirett; Oliver Smith; Sonia Sullivan.

Picture Agency Credits
t=top; b=bottom; c=centre; l=left; r=right
Bruce Coleman Ltd: 28c; Image Bank: 15cl, 15c, 15bc;
Spectrum Colour Library: 15tl, 15tr; Zefa: 14tc, 14cl, 14br.

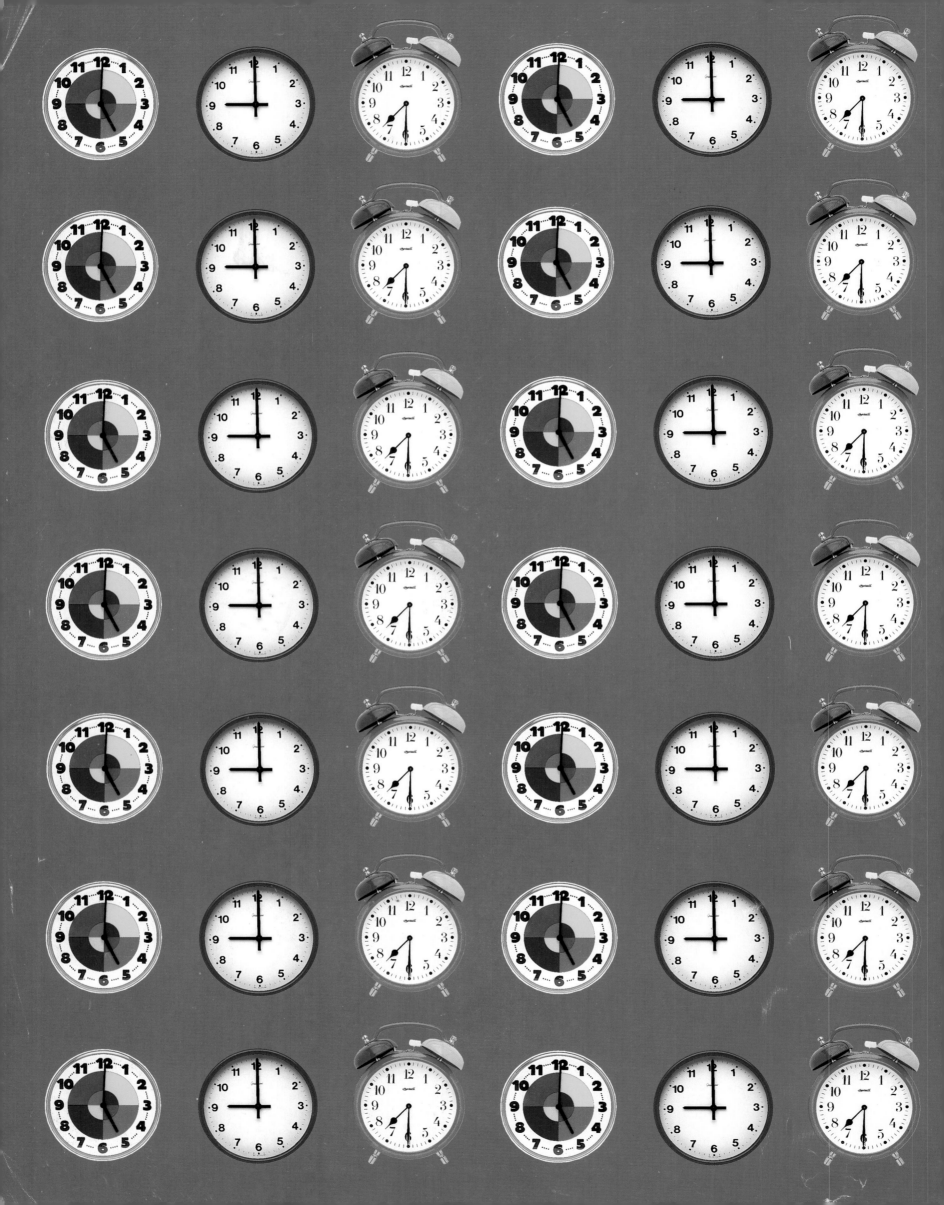